Guatemala

IMMIGRATION TODAY

Maya Logan

PICTURE CREDITS

Cover: Guatemalan-American woman practicing her traditional weaving skills, Miccosukee Indian Village, southern Florida © Nik Wheeler/Corbis/Tranz.

Page 1 © 2006 Kayte Deioma; page 4 (left) © Ted Spiegel/ Corbis/Tranz; page 4 (right) © 2006 Kayte Deioma; page 5 (top) © Bettmann/Corbis/Tranz; page 5 (bottom) © Stock Central; page 6 © Photolibrary; page 8 © Carlos Lopez-Barillas/Corbis/Tranz; page 9 © Photolibrary; page 11 © Keith Dannemiller/Corbis/Tranz; page 12 © Robert Sullivan/AFP Photo/AAP; page 13 (top) © Photolibrary; page 13 (bottom), Corbis; page 14 © Jeff Greenberg/ The Image Works/AAP; page 15 © Sandy Felsenthal/Corbis/Tranz; page 16 © Hector MATA/AFP Photo/AAP; page 22 (top) © Dave G. Houser/Post-Houserstock/Corbis/Tranz; page 22 (bottom) © Andrew Aguilar; page 24 © Audrius Tomonis/www.banknotes.com; page 25 (left and top right) © Carlos Lopez-Barillas/Corbis/Tranz; page 25 (bottom right) © STR/AFP/Getty Images; page 26 (top) © Paul A. Souders/Corbis/Tranz; page 26 (bottom) © Arvind Garg/ Corbis/Tranz; page 29 © David R. Frazier/DanitaDelimont.com.

Produced through the worldwide resources of the National Geographic Society, John M. Fahey, Jr., President and Chief Executive Officer; Gilbert M. Grosvenor, Chairman of the Board.

PREPARED BY NATIONAL GEOGRAPHIC SCHOOL PUBLISHING
Sheron Long, Chief Executive Officer; Samuel Gesumaria, President; Steve Mico, Executive Vice President and Publisher; Francis Downey, Editor in Chief; Richard Easby, Editorial Manager; Margaret Sidlosky, Director of Design and Illustrations; Jim Hiscott, Design Manager; Cynthia Olson and Ruth Ann Thompson, Art Directors; Matt Wascavage, Director of Publishing Services; Lisa Pergolizzi, Production Manager.

MANUFACTURING AND QUALITY CONTROL
Christopher A. Liedel, Chief Financial Officer; Phillip L. Schlosser, Vice President; Clifton M. Brown III, Director.

EDITOR
Mary Anne Wengel

PROGRAM CONSULTANTS
Dr. Shirley V. Dickson, National Literacy Consultant; Margit E. McGuire, Ph.D., Professor of Teacher Education and Social Studies, Seattle University.

National Geographic Theme Sets program developed by Macmillan Education Australia Pty Limited.

Published by the National Geographic Society
1145 17th Street, N.W.
Washington, D.C. 20036-4688

ISBN: 978-1-4263-5178-5

Printed in Hong Kong.

2011 2010 2009 2008 2007
2 3 4 5 6 7 8 9 10 11 12 13 14 15

Contents

Immigration to the United States

Immigrants are people who leave their own country to go and live in another country. People have been immigrating to the United States for hundreds of years. New immigrants arrive each year. They make the United States their home. Today, many Americans can trace their roots back to another country. Ukraine, Guatemala, Jamaica, and Vietnam are some of the countries new immigrants come from.

Key Concepts

1. People choose to immigrate for many different reasons.
2. People who immigrate face many challenges.
3. People who immigrate contribute to the life and culture of the United States.

Four Groups of Immigrants

Ukrainian

Ukrainian immigrants come from Ukraine in Europe.

Guatemalan

Guatemalan immigrants come from Guatemala in Central America.

In this book you will learn about people who immigrate from Guatemala.

Jamaican

Jamaican immigrants come from Jamaica in the Caribbean.

Vietnamese

Vietnamese immigrants come from Vietnam in Asia.

Immigration from Guatemala

Imagine living through years of war. There is violence around you. Life is also hard because you are poor. You do not have a job. It is hard to survive. Would you leave your country to seek a better life? Many people have left Guatemala. They have come to the United States. They hope they will find a better life here.

Guatemala

Guatemala is a country in Central America. For many years there was a war in Guatemala. Many people were hurt. Thousands of people died in the war. Guatemala was not a safe place to live. In 1996, the war ended.

Thousands of people celebrated the end of the war.

Many people want to leave Guatemala. Many people are poor. They suffered during the war. Some of these people have moved to the United States. They traveled here by land and by sea.

Look at the map below to see where Guatemala is.

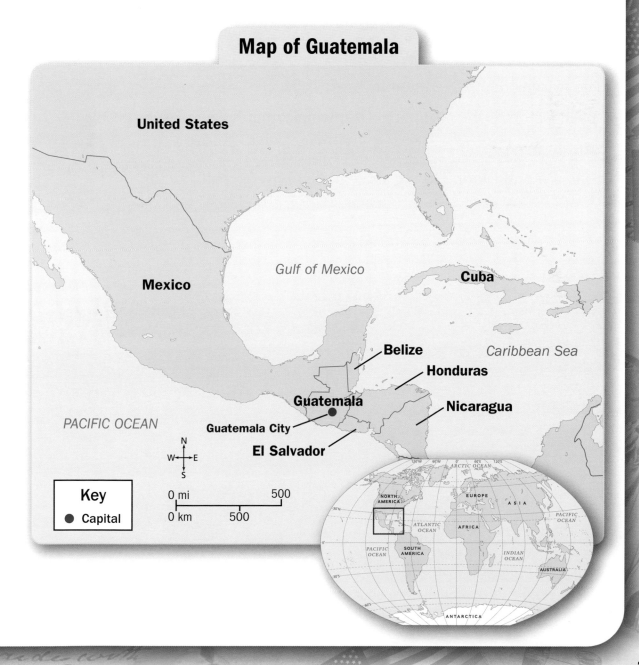

Map of Guatemala

Key Concept 1 People choose to immigrate for many different reasons.

Why People Immigrate

People who leave their country to live in another country are called immigrants. People **immigrate** for many reasons. Some people leave their country because they are unhappy with their way of life.

immigrate
to move to a new country to live

The reasons that make them leave are called "push factors." One push factor is **unemployment.** The reasons people want to move to a new place are called "pull factors." The chance to get a job is a pull factor. Having a safe place to live is a pull factor.

Many people in Guatemala are poor. Some make a little money by recycling trash.

Leaving Guatemala

Many Guatemalans left their country to get away from the war. War and fear were the main push factors. Many Guatemalans came to the United States as **refugees.**

Poverty is another push factor. Guatemala has a weak **economy.** There are many poor people in Guatemala. Many people do not earn much money. Others do not have a job at all. Many of these people decide to move. They hope to find a job in a new place.

Many farmers in Guatemala are poor. This Guatemalan farmer's crop has failed because of a drought.

Coming to the United States

People are pulled to immigrate to the United States. The United States is a rich country. People can live well here. There are good schools here. There are more jobs here than in Guatemala. People can earn more money here. The United States is a more peaceful place to live too.

Family ties are a strong pull factor. Many people move to the United States to join members of their family who already live here.

Look at the bar graph. It shows you how many people from Guatemala immigrated to the United States between 1986 and 2004.

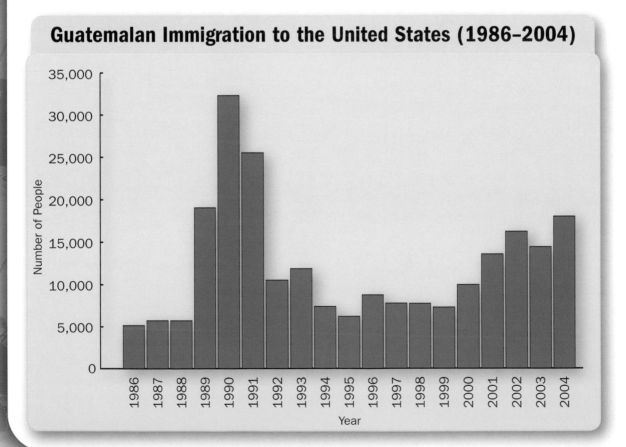

Guatemalan Immigration to the United States (1986–2004)

The Challenges of Immigration

New immigrants face **challenges.** The first is how
to reach the new country. Most Guatemalans come
to the United States as refugees. Some travel
overland. They cross the country of Mexico. They
then reach the United States border. Others travel
by boat. They sail across the Gulf of Mexico. The
journey to the United States can be long and hard.

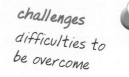

*challenges
difficulties to
be overcome*

During the war it was against the law to leave Guatemala. Sometimes
the army caught people trying to leave. The army forced them to go back
to their homes.

The army caught these Guatemalan children and their parents trying to escape
from Guatemala in 1993.

Learning New Ways

Learning to live in a new country is a challenge. Life in Guatemala is very different from life here. Many Guatemalans do not speak English. They speak Mayan or Spanish. To get by in the United States, they have to learn English.

Many immigrants come from small villages. Big cities can seem scary to them. They are not used to tall buildings and crowded streets. Phones and computers may be new to them. In the United States, they have to learn new ways to do things. They have to learn how to shop and get around. They also have to find a job.

These Guatemalan children are learning English.

Fitting into American Life

Immigrants have to work hard to get used to a new life. Many Guatemalan immigrants face **discrimination.** Sometimes, they do not get jobs because they are different. They may not get jobs because they do not speak English well. Discrimination is against the law in the United States. But it still happens.

New immigrants can be lonely. They leave their friends and family behind. It may be hard to make new friends in their new country.

Children who leave Guatemala will miss the friends they leave behind.

There are students from many different countries in American schools.

Joining American Society

Today, there are many people from Guatemala who live in the United States. They **contribute** to American society in many ways.

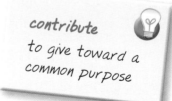

contribute
to give toward a
common purpose

All immigrants contribute to the economy. They do this by working and paying **taxes.** Immigrants do many jobs. Some have their own businesses. They own travel agencies, grocery stores, and gas stations. Some work as gardeners and cleaners. Others work in factories and restaurants.

This Guatemalan woman is selling handicrafts at a market in Florida.

Keeping Guatemalan Culture Alive

People from Guatemala blend in, yet they keep their own **culture** alive. They do this in many ways.

Many Guatemalans like to speak their own language when they are at home. They like to listen to radio shows in their own language. By doing these things, they keep their language alive.

Some people open restaurants that serve Guatemalan food. Some dishes, such as tamales, have become popular.

Two girls wearing Guatemalan costumes at a parade

15

Immigrants also celebrate their festivals in the United States. The Day of the Dead and Semana Santa, or Easter Week, are popular. People put on plays and parades.

During Easter Week, some families make pictures with flower petals and sawdust. The Day of the Dead in November is important too. On this day, people remember loved ones who have died. They make paper puppets and skeleton costumes. In these ways, Guatemalans keep their culture alive.

People wear colorful costumes and masks on the Day of the Dead.

Think About the **Key Concepts**

Think about what you read. Think about the pictures and diagrams. Use these to answer the questions. Share what you think with others.

1. What pushes people to immigrate to the United States? What pulls them?

2. What challenges do immigrants face to get to a new country?

3. What do immigrants have to do to fit into a new country?

4. How does the immigrant group in this book keep their culture alive?

Bar Graph

Bar graphs are used to compare different amounts.

A bar graph uses bars to show amounts being compared. Look back at the bar graph on page 10. It shows the number of Guatemalan immigrants who came to the United States from 1986 to 2004. Each bar shows the number of people who immigrated that year.

The graph on page 19 is also a bar graph. It shows the number of immigrants from four countries in 2004. The bar graph allows you to compare the number of people in each group.

How to Read a Bar Graph

1. Read the title.
The title tells you what information the bar graph shows.

2. Read the key.
The key tells you what information is being compared.

3. Get the general idea.
On the bar graph, the taller bars represent a greater quantity than the shorter bars.

4. Get the details.
Look at the numbers on the vertical line, or axis. Match that number with the top of each bar. These numbers help you figure out the quantity each bar represents.

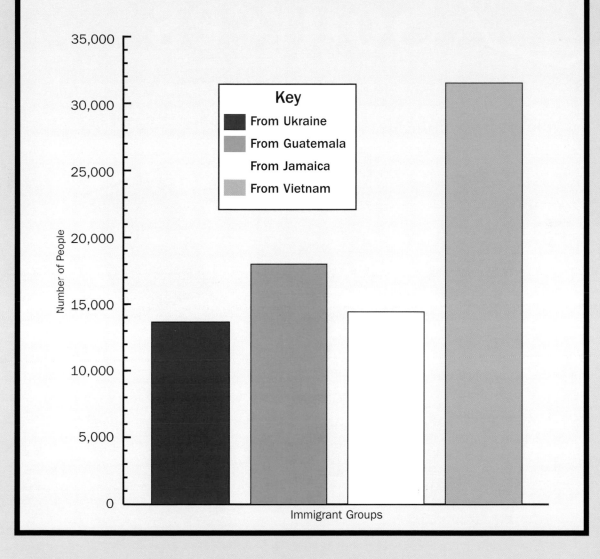

Immigration to the United States (2004)

Key
- From Ukraine
- From Guatemala
- From Jamaica
- From Vietnam

Number of People

Immigrant Groups

What Does the Bar Graph Show?

Read the bar graph above. How many people arrived in the United States from each country in 2004? Which group had the largest number of immigrants? Which group had the smallest number? Tell a classmate what you learned from this bar graph.

Reference Sources

The purpose of **reference sources** is to inform. Reference sources can take many forms.

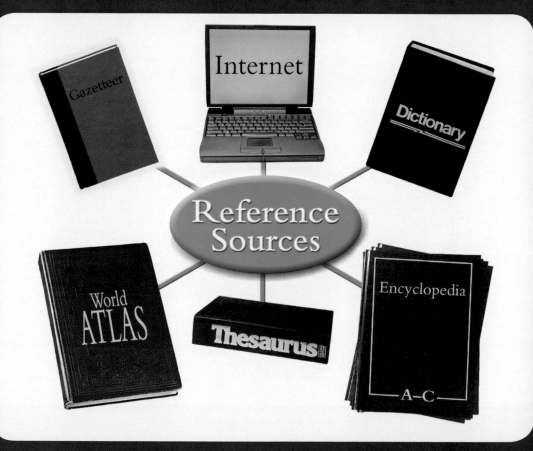

You use different reference sources for different things. For example, if you want to know how to spell *immigration,* use a dictionary. But if you want to know geographical facts about a country, use a **gazetteer.**

You do not read a reference source from beginning to end. You read only the parts that cover topics you want to learn about.

Guatemala
GAZETTEER

The **title** tells you which country the gazetteer is about.

The amount of land a country covers

Area

Headings name topics.

Guatemala is 42,042 square miles (108,889 square kilometers).

Text gives information about the topic.

Location

Guatemala is a country in Central America. It is between the Pacific Ocean and the Caribbean Sea. It borders four countries.

Maps, photographs, or **diagrams** support the text.

Where a country is in the world and what Is around it

Map of Guatemala

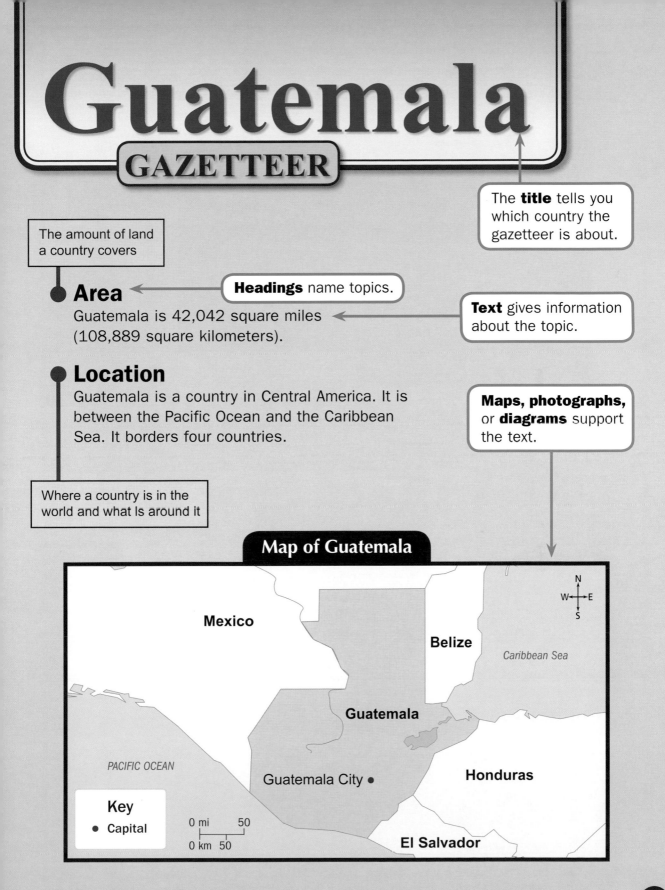

Mexico

Belize

Caribbean Sea

Guatemala

PACIFIC OCEAN

Guatemala City ●

Honduras

Key
● Capital

0 mi   50
0 km   50

El Salvador

N
W — E
S

21

Capital

The capital of Guatemala is Guatemala City.

The city where a country's government has its main office

The National Palace is located in Guatemala City.

Major Cities

Major cities in Guatemala are
- Guatemala City
- Quetzaltenango
- Escuintla

Flag

The Guatemalan flag has three stripes. It has a coat of arms. A coat of arms is made up of the symbols of a country. The Guatemalan coat of arms has a wreath, a scroll, rifles, swords, and a bird called the quetzal.

Population

The total number of people in an area

The population of Guatemala is 12,293,545 (2006).

Natural Features ●────

The physical geography of a country

Guatemala has three main regions. One region is the highlands. Another is a tropical area along both coasts. The final region is tropical jungle in the northern lowlands.

Guatemala has many mountains and volcanoes. Sometimes there are earthquakes. Guatemala has several lakes. Volcanoes formed many of the lakes.

Climate

It is hot and wet in the lowlands. It is cooler in the highlands. The Caribbean coast is often hit by hurricanes.

The Pacific coast is hot year round. Temperatures are around 100° Fahrenheit (38° Celsius).

The bar graph below shows the average rainfall and temperature in the capital, Guatemala City. It is inland, in the southern highlands.

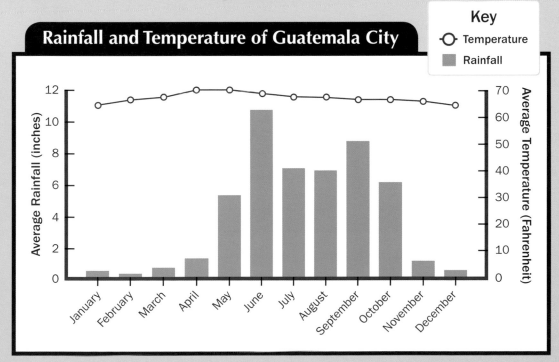

Rainfall and Temperature of Guatemala City

Key
- Temperature
- Rainfall

Industry

Guatemala has many resources and industries. Guatemala makes textiles, clothing, furniture, and chemicals. They also have oil, metals, and rubber. Tourism is also an important industry in Guatemala.

Agriculture ●————

> Farm products the country produces

People in Guatemala grow many crops. These include sugarcane, corn, bananas, coffee, and the spice cardamom.

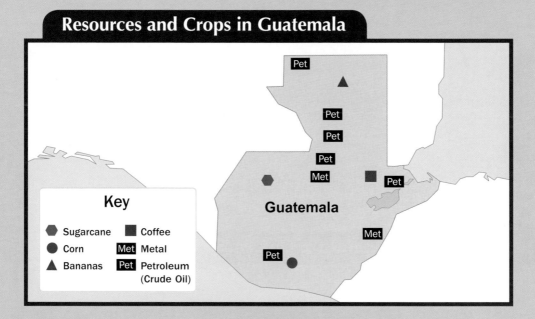

Resources and Crops in Guatemala

Guatemala

Key

- ⬡ Sugarcane
- ● Corn
- ▲ Bananas
- ◼ Coffee
- **Met** Metal
- **Pet** Petroleum (Crude Oil)

Exports ●————

> Goods a country sells to other countries

Guatemala sells some of its products to other countries. These include coffee, sugar, bananas, fruits, and vegetables.

Currency ●————

> The name of the money people use in a country

The currency of Guatemala is the Quetzal.

A 50 Quetzal note

Guatemalan Celebrations

Guatemalans celebrate many festivals. Easter is an important religious festival. Guatemalans celebrate many important dates by flying giant kites.

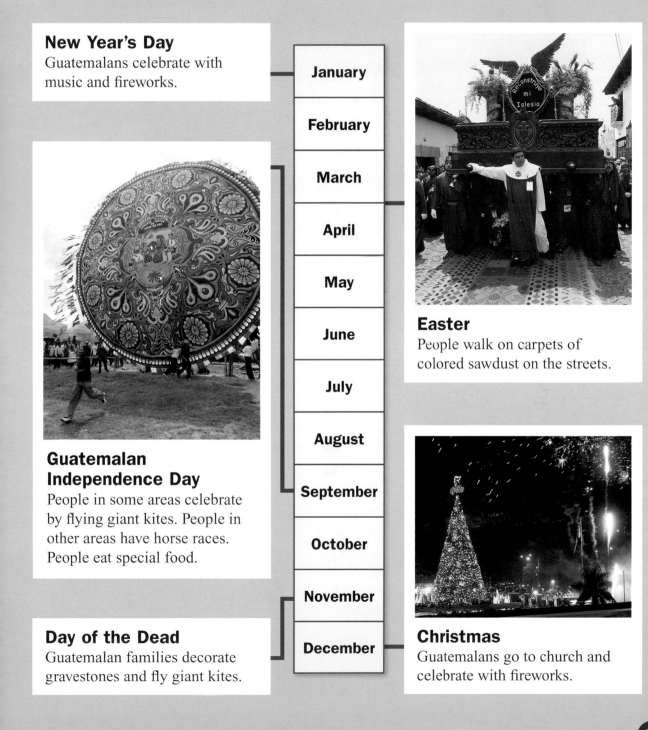

New Year's Day
Guatemalans celebrate with music and fireworks.

Guatemalan Independence Day
People in some areas celebrate by flying giant kites. People in other areas have horse races. People eat special food.

Day of the Dead
Guatemalan families decorate gravestones and fly giant kites.

January
February
March
April
May
June
July
August
September
October
November
December

Easter
People walk on carpets of colored sawdust on the streets.

Christmas
Guatemalans go to church and celebrate with fireworks.

Religion

Most Guatemalan people are Christians. Many are Roman Catholics. A small number of Guatemalans practice traditional Mayan religions.

The Cathedral of Santiago in Antigua, Guatemala

Food

Some Guatemalan traditional dishes are
- tobic (a beef and cabbage soup)
- chicken pepian (chicken cooked in a pumpkin)
- kilim (chicken served with rice and potatoes)
- tortilla (round, flat bread)

Languages

Most Guatemalan people speak Spanish. Many people speak Mayan.

This Guatemalan woman is making tortillas.

Apply the Key Concepts

Key Concept 1 People choose to immigrate for many different reasons.

Activity

Create a concept web. Write down the things that make people decide to immigrate. Include reasons that push people to move from Guatemala. Also include reasons that pull people to the United States.

No Jobs

Reason to Immigrate

Key Concept 2 People who immigrate face many challenges.

Activity

Make a list of the challenges new immigrants may face when they move to the United States. If you were a new immigrant, how would you overcome these challenges? Create an action plan of things you would do to settle and fit into a new country.

Action Plan
1. Take English lessons
2.
3.

Key Concept 3 People who immigrate contribute to the life and culture of the United States.

Activity

Create a poster for a Guatemalan festival. Think about the things that you would enjoy at a festival. Put them on your poster. For example, what food would you bring? What music would you have? Show the festival attractions on the poster.

GUATEMALAN FESTIVAL

Attractions:
•
•

Create Your Own Gazetteer

You have read the gazetteer on Guatemala. Now you can research another country and write a gazetteer for it.

1. Study the Model

Look back at pages 21–26. Think about the type of information a gazetteer contains. How is the gazetteer entry organized? What kinds of headings were used to break the information into easy-to-find sections? What kinds of facts are included about Guatemala? These are the kinds of facts you should include in your gazetteer.

2. Choose a Country

Choose a country you are interested in and would like to know more about. You will now write a gazetteer on that country. Think about the kind of information a reader might look for when using your gazetteer for research. What would a researcher be interested in? This is the type of information you should include in your gazetteer.

Gazetteer Entries

◆ Each entry is about one country.
◆ The title tells us which country the entry is about.
◆ A map helps us locate the country.
◆ The facts tell us important information about the country.
◆ Pictures support the facts and add interest.

3. Research the Topic

Make a list of the kinds of information you will need to find. Use the library or Internet to find the facts and figures you need. Write down all the information that you can use. Look for a map of the country. Look for pictures to include in your gazetteer that support the information you have collected.

Topic: Belize

1. Where is Belize?

2. How many people live there?

3. What are the natural features of the country?

4. Write a Draft

Plan how you are going to organize your gazetteer. Start with a title. The title should name the country you are writing about. Create headings for the different kinds of information you are including. Arrange your headings in the order you would like them to appear. Fit the information you have found under the headings. If you have all the information you need, you can begin writing your gazetteer. If you included pictures, write captions for them.

5. Revise and Edit

Read your draft. Is it easy to quickly see the kinds of information the gazetteer contains? Are all the facts and figures in the gazetteer correct? Look for words that are misspelled. If there are any mistakes, fix them.

Present Your Own Gazetteer

Now you can share your work. Get together with your classmates and put all of your gazetteer entries together into a class gazetteer.

How to Make a Display of Gazetteers

1. Make sure every gazetteer entry has a title.
The title should name the country.

2. Organize all the gazetteer entries alphabetically.
Look at the title of each entry. Put the gazetteer entries in alphabetical order by country.

3. Number the pages.
Add the page number for each page.

4. Prepare a table of contents.
Look at the table of contents in other books. Now make one for your book.

5. Make a cover.
Talk with your classmates about what you all want on the cover. Choose a picture that will tell what the book is about. Then make your cover.

6. Now bind the pages together.
You can staple the pages together. Or you can punch holes on the left side and tie the pages together with yarn.

Glossary

challenges – difficulties to be overcome

contribute – to give toward a common purpose

culture – the traditions, language, dress, ceremonies, and other ways of life that a group of people share

discrimination – unfair treatment of people because of their race, sex, or religion

economy – a system of making, managing, and spending money

immigrate – to move to a new country to live

poverty – the state of being poor

refugees – people who have to leave their country because of war or harsh treatment

taxes – money people must pay to the government

unemployment – the state of not having a job

Index